WHALE HUNTERS WISDOM SERIES
Volume III

RIDING THE WHALE

Adapt Your Sales Strategies
to Close Big Deals

Dr. Barbara Weaver Smith
and The Whale Hunters

BIGGER DEALS
BIGGER CUSTOMERS

www.thewhalehunters.com

© 2007-2016 The Whale Hunters, Inc.

info@thewhalehunters.com

Whale Hunters Wisdom Series

By Dr. Barbara Weaver Smith
and The Whale Hunters

www.thewhalehunters.com

info@thewhalehunters.com

© 2007-2016 The Whale Hunters, Inc.

ISBN: 978-0-9975379-0-1

Published in the United States of America by The Whale Hunters, Inc.

The Whale Hunters
3054 East Bartlett Place
Chandler, AZ 85249
www.thewhalehunters.com
info@thewhalehunters.com

480.584.4012

Preface

Aimed at owners and executives seeking explosive growth for their companies, the *Whale Hunters Wisdom* series offers explanations, tools, personal anecdotes and real life examples to guide you in scouting, hunting, and harvesting "whales," those accounts 10 to 20 times larger than your current average account.

The Whale Hunters Process™ is derived from our study of how the Inuit people of far northwestern Alaska hunted whales. Their story is one of indomitable courage and persistence. A small team of people ventured out into icy waters in a sealskin boat during the dark days of early Spring to capture and then land and harvest the biggest mammal on earth. Their story has the power of truth, and we have great respect and admiration for the Inuit. The dangerous hunt demanded tremendous courage, a special boat and tools, and a ritual that ensured the hunters and villagers would be successful. Why did the whale hunters risk their lives? **One whale will feed the village for an entire year.**

The Whale Hunters, Inc. is a strategic sales and business development company. We teach a process to develop a fast-growth culture within your company. This permanent process integration requires a defined strategy with clear steps, teamwork, defined responsibilities, and a common understanding that the village survives because it hunts.

Through The Whale Hunters Process™, your company will be positioned for explosive growth that can be managed consistently as you land and support whale-sized accounts. Learn more by visiting our website, www.thewhalehunters. com, where you may register to receive the *Whale Hunters Wisdom* newsletter. It's absolutely free.

www.thewhalehunters.com
© 2007-2016 The Whale Hunters, Inc.

info@thewhalehunters.com

The Whale Hunters Process™
A proven, nine-phase process for transforming sales development

Whale Hunting creates a disciplined sales culture in your company that allows you to optimize your ability to land and harvest large accounts. This dramatic shift in thinking and practice precipitates explosive growth of your company's revenues and market position.

Scouting guides you to know, seek and harpoon whales whose business will be ideal for you. It all starts with knowing who you're hunting, with a focus on market and sales research and the creation of a target filter.

Harpoon   Know

Scout

Seek

Celebrate   Beach

Harvest

Honor

Sew   Ride

Hunt

Capture

Harvesting brings sales and operations departments together in an integrated process to ensure you harvest your whale effectively, efficiently and harmoniously. It includes key account management and growing new business with your best accounts.

Hunting focuses on communicating with, presenting to, and securely closing your ideal whale accounts. Our method of progressive discovery and disclosure relies on critical questions at each step of the hunt.

V

Table of Contents

info@thewhalehunters.com

www.thewhalehunters.com
© 2007-2016 The Whale Hunters, Inc.

Introduction

Inuit whale hunters had tremendous respect for the whale they hunted. They understood the whale would be swift, strong, and cunning—trying every trick it knew to rid itself of the harpoon in its blubber and the weight of the boat attached to it. And the whale knew a lot of tricks. Fortunately, the Inuit knew quite a few, too.

When the whale is first harpooned, what it feels is more fear and irritation than pain, and its response is to try to shake that irritation free. This is a very dangerous time for the whale hunters. The whale will respond instantly and with great force. It may dive or it might begin swimming toward the open sea. Whatever it does, it always drags the boat [called an *umiak*] along with it, by means of the rope attached to the harpoon, at astonishingly high speeds.

Once the whale understands that the irritation is not going to go away easily, it will try a more cunning approach. Perhaps it will slow down to a very slow pace and then suddenly speed up, hoping that the sudden difference in speed will shake the irritation loose. The whale's enormous tail could sweep around and throw the *umiak* and its hunters into the frigid Bering Sea waters.

During their long winters, the Inuit taught their children about the whale hunt and shared the history of the whales and the hunts. They never lost focus during their hunt, and incredibly, they were often successful. The key was to understand what might happen and to prepare appropriate responses well in advance of the actual event. Once the hunt begins, there is only time for reaction, not for reflection.

2

Businesses looking for rapid, sustainable growth will find themselves in an analogous situation. While the whale-sized companies you are pursuing will probably not act in such an immediately energetic manner, they will certainly be reacting with fear because something new will be expected from them. This volume of the *Whale Hunters Wisdom Series* will help you understand why companies behave the way they do in the middle of your sales process and what you can do about it. In this volume, The Whale Hunters share their experiences and reflect on what it is like to ride the whale to successful completion of the hunt.

www.thewhalehunters.com
© 2007-2016 The Whale Hunters, Inc.

info@thewhalehunters.com

Much like the proverbial elephant scared of a mouse, whale companies are afraid, too. They fear change, conflict, work, and failure. Your job is to alleviate these fears and move toward advantage. We provide recommendations to do just that.

4

Stop Scaring Whales

It is hard to believe you could scare a whale. Whales are huge, strong, and much more powerful than you are, right? But when you look into the culture of a whale-sized organization, you may find a fearful place harboring fearful people. They scare easily, so your job is to alleviate their fear.

Whale cultures can be maddening to smaller, more entrepreneurial companies. How many times have you been selling into a whale-sized company and left meetings or phone calls shaking your head because the whale could not or would not make a decision that was so clearly in its best interests? How can you explain their reluctance? How can you bring them to a decision?

As we have said before, the nature of whales is to seek safety over benefit. For that reason, fear trumps all other emotions in their process of making a decision. Smaller companies that sell to whales usually tout the benefits they will provide, with little attention to the whale's fears. Therefore, they often make mistakes during their sales process that create fear in the whale and lead to unsuccessful hunts. To hunt more successfully, you must learn how to stop scaring whales.

www.thewhalehunters.com
© 2007-2016 The Whale Hunters, Inc.

info@thewhalehunters.com

Whales fear four circumstances:

Change. Any variation from what they are doing now

Conflict. Any disruption of the relationships, be they inter- or intra-departmental, between the whale and customers, or between the whale and current suppliers

Work. Any additional expenditure of effort or activity in the current workload of the people with whom you are meeting

Failure. Mistakes, shortcomings, problems, or any other public signs of a bad decision

Do you feel stuck here? If you are selling anything significant (typical of a whale-sized deal), you inevitably create at least one of these circumstances and usually more than one. From a whale hunting perspective, you need specific tactics to reduce the whale's fears so that the whale can be ready to hear your benefits.

Here are our recommendations to counter fear and move toward advantage:

Get everyone to the "Buyers' Table." This is our term for the entire group who participates over the course of many meetings when you are working through a long sales process with a whale. Everyone who will be impacted by the whale's buying decision must be at the table, since you cannot educate or calm people with whom you are not connected. If any department or a group may be impacted negatively by working with your company, it is better to hear them out and work through the issues than to avoid their concerns.

6

Devote a 90:10 effort to a 50:50 commitment. Declare early and often that if the whale will make its portion of the commitment, you will take more than your share of the implementation responsibility. You might offer to provide extra training resources from your company, backup tooling and engineering, or delivery schedules that are outside of your normal way of doing business. Regardless of what it is, you have to be able to show the whale that the effort on your side will be enough to take a lot of the transition burden off of the whale.

Reinforce the status quo. Make certain that the whale clearly understands which of its many systems will not change as a consequence of doing a deal with you. All complex systems, such as accounting, procurement, supply chain management, training, manufacturing, and so on, require a great deal of effort to modify, as well as great risk of interruption if something does not work. Highlight regularly how your solution will not change these systems, and you will make the whale feel more at ease with you.

Propose small steps leading to long plans. Build a plan with incremental ramp-in and clearly defined performance thresholds for continuing and growing the relationship. It is easier to get a whale to take a series of smaller steps than to buy in to the entire relationship plan.

Spread it out. Demonstrate that you can dedicate more people, more resources, and more time than your competitors. In considering a purchase from a smaller company, the whale likes the idea that it will have leverage in the relationship as well as access to your company's best and brightest. However, it also fears that your company might be too small to deliver. Showing the strength of your people, your resources, and your

www.thewhalehunters.com
© 2007-2016 The Whale Hunters, Inc.

info@thewhalehunters.com

time commitments during the sales process will help the whale to feel comfortable in choosing to do business with you.

Finally, try asking these questions to get the whale's fears out on the table early.

> • If we were signing the contract to do work together today, who from your company would have to be in the room?
>
> • Who in your company might be negatively impacted if you changed what you are doing now and started using us?
>
> • Tell me about the on-boarding of the last provider/partner/vendor/supplier to your company from the outside; and what were the biggest issues?
>
> • When you have worked with firms like ours in the past, what have been the biggest snafus you have had to deal with?

Their answers should guide your sales plan. You will know who needs to be at the Buyers' Table, what departments have the most to lose, how to calm their fears about problems in the past, and where their biggest fears reside about buying from a small company.

You are smaller than a whale, and that size differential is what most scares the whale in a business dealing with you. Stop scaring whales, and your business will grow dramatically.

8

Reflection

With your team, identify things about your company that might scare a much bigger company.

Fear of Change (Hiring you requires them to do things differently)

_____

_____

Fear of Conflict (Internal conflict over hiring you)

_____

_____

Fear of Work (Hiring you causes them more work)

_____

_____

Fear of Failure (Making a Mistake)

_____

_____

info@thewhalehunters.com

www.thewhalehunters.com
© 2007-2016 The Whale Hunters, Inc.

ACTION

Make a list of the most significant fears that you identified. Then develop one or more "fear busters" for each. A fear buster is something tangible that you can present to a whale to alleviate fear—a chart, testimonial, white paper, graphic, reference, team biography, etc.

Fear   **Fear Buster**

_____   _____

_____   _____

_____   _____

_____   _____

_____   _____

_____   _____

_____   _____

_____   _____

_____   _____

_____   _____

_____   _____

_____   _____

10

The Rolling Stones might have declared that "time, time, time is on my side," but time is NOT on the side of the whale hunter! Dangers are associated with moving too quickly and too slowly through the sales process. What to do? Maintain the proper pace. Here's how.

11

Time Kills All Deals

In the movie *Speed*, Sandra Bullock is aboard a bus that must maintain a constant speed. If the bus goes too fast or too slow, a bomb will be triggered, killing all on board.

Complex sales are often equally dangerous and out of control. Sometimes the buyer is attempting to purchase services faster than you can sell. Other times, the process has stalled and a deal may not occur at all. Whether it is too fast or too slow, each offers a series of challenges for the harpooners and village.

Nothing makes a harpooner happier than when the client says "yes" and punctuates that affirmation with a signed contract. However, from time to time, your buyer wants to begin the relationship before you are ready to fulfill the sale. Particularly in the case of complex sales, a client's urgency can outstrip its capacity to perform at a high level of excellence.

The risks associated with the "fast yes":

- An inability to develop a proper plan for implementation.

- Lack of operational capacity.

- An insufficient or underdeveloped scope of work leading to substantially changed orders or missed opportunity.

- A bias to bypass pre-sale processes including credit checks, use of a target filter, and completed estimating.

- A disenfranchised operational team due to lack of sufficient time for proper "buy-in."

12

Good harpooners have a sense for when a deal has stalled. But often harpooners underestimate the risk of this behavior and do not properly adjust tactics.

If a deal begins to stall, you are vulnerable to these risks:

- Members of the boat can become disinterested and sloppy in their execution of the sales process.

- The client organization may have objections that it is unwilling to share, causing follow-up to be inappropriate to the client's real needs.

- You may give in to a tendency to push the process by offering discounts or overselling.

- A stall can be perceived prematurely as a "no" and the boat can disband out of a false belief that a deal is no longer possible.

- The parameters of the initial pricing may change and now the organization has to either bid unprofitably or the bid is no longer competitive.

www.thewhalehunters.com
© 2007-2016 The Whale Hunters, Inc.
info@thewhalehunters.com

Keeping your eye on the "proper pace"

The Whale Hunters Process™ focuses on closing big deals. Proper pace is important in creating deals that work for both parties. Too fast, and it is likely the sales organization will be burned or the client will be underserved. Too slow, and the likelihood to close falls at a startling rate or the organization's inclination to overreach manifests itself.

Ideally, pace is something that you anticipate and control through multiple steps:

Step 1: Agree on the sales process. As basic as this may sound, many organizations fail to inform their prospect as to how the process should move forward. Or the client may present a timeline that you fail to question or to verify their intent.

Step 2: Write the process down and share it with your client, including timelines. Putting things in writing does not guarantee compliance. However, the gentle reminder of a written document, appropriately shared in both organizations, creates an implied sense of obligation unless challenged at inception. It also notifies the client of your schedule for acceptance of the opportunity, avoiding the possibility of the client jumping the gun.

Step 3: Validate each step and foreshadow as you go along. In The Whale Hunters Process™, each significant movement is tracked, measured, and validated. Work with the prospect to confirm the completed step and immediately follow up with the next anticipated milestone.

Step 4: Promptly renegotiate missed dates. Often a client will move back the timeline, and say, "I am not sure when we will get to the next step." A good harpooner will not let this go at face value. Real questions like these will have to be answered:

- "Will the project still occur?"

- "Will your organization be re-bidding this project?"

- "Have you narrowed the field, and how do we stand?"

- "What can we do to be helpful during the interim while you still have this need but no agreed-upon solution?"

Step 5: Be willing to walk away. The hardest thing a harpooner has to do is cut the line on a whale that makes no sense for the village. However, a whale that will damage the boat, risk the crew, or become too heavy to tow back to shore is not a whale worth taking.

Learn to manage the pace and you will increase your rate of success.

15

Reflection

With your team, reflect on past deals from the following perspectives.

Deals that we pursued too long (should have known they were/are dead):

_____

_____

_____

_____

Signs that we missed or ignored:

_____

_____

_____

_____

In retrospect, steps that we could have taken?

_____

_____

_____

_____

Action

Review your current pipeline. Identify whale-deals that are currently stalled.

-
-
-
-
-

Create an action plan for each stalled deal.

_____

_____

_____

Build time parameters into your sales process. For example, from Step I to Step II "ought to take" three weeks, or 15 days, etc. Include this in your sales management tools (which may be as simple as a spreadsheet) and review in sales meetings or with your leadership team.

_____

_____

_____

_____

And remember—Time Kills All Deals!

Stepping out of your comfort zone and onto the dance floor with a whale? This takes guts! It also requires a solid understanding of the scope of the opportunity and access to the right people. Got all three of these? It's time to boogie!

18

Dancing with Whales

Go to a ninth grade dance and you will see a clear illustration of one of the biggest challenges in sales: the opening conversation. Boys lined up on one side of the gym, girls on the other, and snowflakes of light dancing off the mirrored spinning ball landing on everyone. The best looking, most athletic, smartest – fill in your adjectives, it doesn't matter – are all up against the wall, not on the dance floor. Their minds are filled with doubt, not knowing what to talk about or how to approach the other person, and fearing rejection.

Those who do dance are kids who know each other well. Perhaps they grew up together, have classes and labs together, or share extracurricular activities. They dance to dance, not necessarily out of a high level of interest in each other. Sometimes they even spend the whole dance plotting together how one will introduce the other to the person in whom they are really interested.

Like the young dancers, salespeople within your company sell where they are the most comfortable. That is in a peer-to- peer relationship or a near-peer relationship. The CEO of a small company may sell to the CEO or other officer of another small company. But your sales vice president may be a nearer-peer to the purchasing agent than to a large corporation's VP.

Even if your company has made a habit of selling to larger companies and proudly displays the logos of all of the Fortune 1000 clients you have, often or even usually you are doing small amounts of business with those firms and usually with divisions, sub-divisions, small regions, or single locations. The size similarity means familiarity, and that makes everyone comfortable.

Tiny work with a large company is not what whale hunting is all about. Whale hunting is all about whale-sized work. To accomplish whale-sized work, a firm must become comfortable initiating the dance with a stranger. This does not necessarily mean changing target industries, territories, or markets. It does mean changing your orientation away from peer and near-peer interactions to sales opportunities that are bigger and less familiar.

Whales buy differently and for different reasons than small companies. For example:

- Whales have big problems, so they purchase big solutions.

- Whale organizations are complex, so they take time to make their purchases and involve many of their own people in the decision.

- Whale changes are big. Any change to the way they do business, like a new vendor, has ripples that are felt throughout their operations. Thus, they are cautious and want to know as much as possible about who will be involved and how they will be doing business with you.

Step 1: Scope of Opportunity – solve whale-sized problems. If you sell office supplies, you will talk to secretaries who buy paper clips. If you sell centralized ordering of office supplies, you will talk to procurement officers and budget monitors. But if you sell office expense reduction through office supply inventory control, you will talk to the COO, CFO, or CEO.

info@thewhalehunters.com

These distinctions are not just issues of different language meaning the same thing. They are issues of what size problem you propose to solve and the value it delivers. A company with 10 locations needs someone to handle its office supply inventory management, not another vendor of paper clips. Even if you offer paper clips in 20 colors, 10 sizes, and 5% lower in cost, you are solving too small a problem to be of value. Sell paper clips and there is little wonder why you talk to secretaries.

Step 2: Point of Entry – talk to people who have whale-sized needs. It is a cliché in the world of sales to "start as high as you can in the prospect organization." That is a universal belief. However, more important than higher is who. Who has the vantage point to see a whale-sized opportunity for your firm inside of their company? Now, who has the power to convene and guide the sales process in their company if he or she believes that you can solve a big need?

The final decision-maker is not the most important person in the complex sale. Rather, you are looking for the person who can point out the people most rewarded and protected for saying "no" to your company. Your sales process and initial point of contact need to be aimed at the most knowledgeable people in a company for understanding the whale's needs, not necessarily the most powerful economic buyer.

Step 3: Confidence – the whale hunter's confidence. I have been a big fan of the great NFL quarterback Peyton Manning. I like what he says about pressure: "Pressure is what you feel when you don't know what you are going to do next." That one is worth reading again.

Whales are not particularly forgiving or patient. They expect potential partners who are selling to them to have a clear understanding of their needs and a path for presenting a solution. All of the contacts will expect you to articulate specifically your process for developing a solution and to present a compelling proposal. If you are going to enter into new waters, you have to have the confidence that only a detailed plan, ample preparation, and careful rehearsal can give you. In front of the prospective whale is not the place to "wing it." Develop and understand your case beforehand.

It has been more than a few years since middle school for all of us. We are out of the gym and have more invested than a five-minute dance in knowing how to open the conversation and pick the right partner.

So write your script, choreograph your steps, rehearse with friends, and ask that whale to dance.

Visit our website now to claim your free list of CEO membership organizations!
http://thewhalehunters.com/CEOlist

www.thewhalehunters.com
© 2007-2016 The Whale Hunters, Inc.   info@thewhalehunters.com

Reflection

What do we sell that solves whale-sized problems?

_____

_____

_____

_____

Do you and your team display the confidence to pursue to longer, more complex, and more difficult sales?

_____

_____

_____

_____

Do you have the right criteria to target and hunt whales?

_____

_____

_____

_____

info@thewhalehunters.com

www.thewhalehunters.com
© 2007-2016 The Whale Hunters, Inc.

Action

1. Clarify your message to the whales. This means conducting a Brand Audit and defining the unique characteristics that set you apart from your competitors.

_____

_____

_____

_____

2. Learn how to find warm leads and warm introductions to whale prospects.

_____

_____

_____

_____

3. Implement a required rehearsal plan for proposals.

_____

_____

_____

_____

A whale may express curiosity, attention, and desire to learn more. And oh, how flattering such expressions may be! But whale hunters are wise to learn those patterns of whale behavior that really matter: investment, commitment, and interest.

The Buying Pattern

"A cloud does not know why it moves in just such a direction and at such a speed
. . . It feels an impulsion . . . this is the place to go now. But the sky knows the
reasons and the patterns behind all clouds, and you will know, too, when you lift
yourself high enough to see beyond horizons." – Richard Bach

Horizon is not a destination. It moves away as you try to draw nearer. Always,
on the open sea, your destination lies beyond a horizon. In your small boat, with
rudimentary guidance tools, how do you decide when to pursue a whale, when to
change course, or when to head for home? Seek to find the pattern behind the
clouds. Expressions of curiosity, attention, and education may give you an impulse
to go in such a direction. But in a whale hunt, the pattern you must know is
investment, commitment, and interest.

Investment more than curiosity

Information is the coin of the whale-hunting realm. If the Buyers' Table withholds
information, limits your access to informed people, or won't share context that will
make your conversations solution-oriented, your whale is unwilling to invest. The
whale may be curious to learn more about what you know, but after a slow and
painful process you are unlikely to beach this whale. If, however, the buyers give
you relevant information, explain the context of their business issues, and ask you
probing questions, they are expressing investment in the process, not just curiosity.

Gather this kind of information early in your sales process to be confident that the
whale's goals are aligned with yours:

Buying process: What is the process that the whale will use to bring on board a new provider and a new solution? Can you win in that process?

Fears: Who will be most negatively impacted in their company by choosing to do business with you? What systems, processes, and personnel will experience the most change? Can you talk to these people and understand their fears?

Pain: What are the core issues around the whale's desire to change? Is this a pain that your solution can cure?

Buyers' Table: Who are the polar bears, caribou, and even the eels in this deal? Will they meet with the subject matter experts on your boat?

Commitment more than attendance

You know that people are interested if they keep showing up and they bring the right kinds of friends. Whales demonstrate commitment when more people, new people, and people who will implement your solution come to your meetings and participate in your communication. Assess commitment by these criteria:

Responsibility levels of attendees: Are people from higher levels in the whale being recruited to meetings with you? If you are being introduced to more people but not climbing the decision-making tree, you are giving away consulting and market intelligence rather than generating commitment to buy. Monitor your proximity to decision-makers.

Predictability: If people cancel meetings with you or simply fail to show up, or if several unexpected people are in the room, the whale is demonstrating a lack of commitment to you and your process. Don't kid yourself about their excuses.

Interaction: Are the people in the room engaging in dialog with you? Are they asking tough questions? Are they discussing your solution in terms of their needs? Assess the quality of your conversations.

Interest rather than just education

Time kills all deals. We know that when you are hunting a whale, time rarely works in your favor. Buyers often need to educate themselves on market alternatives in order to justify a choice that they have already made. However, if the whale is engaged and interested, the buyers move forward in their relationships with you. How do you know?

Time between sales process steps: If the time between process steps stretches out beyond your expectations, you will most likely lose.

Time between promises and delivery: Whale-sized deals require lots of information and involvement on the part of the whale. In many of the sales steps, both you and the whale walk away with commitments made to each other. A whale that consistently misses commitment dates doesn't return inquiries, and pushes back delivery dates demonstrates a fundamental lack of interest.

www.thewhalehunters.com
© 2007-2016 The Whale Hunters, Inc.   info@thewhalehunters.com

On the open ocean, you see horizon in all directions and no land at all. You need navigation tools to help you assess progress towards your destination. The "pattern behind all clouds" is process. If you define your process, track your progress along that process, and change course when the process isn't working, you will come to understand the wisdom of the sky.

Visit our website now to claim your free list of CEO membership organizations!
http://thewhalehunters.com/CEOlist

info@thewhalehunters.com   www.thewhalehunters.com
                                  © 2007-2016 The Whale Hunters, Inc.

Reflection

With your team, brainstorm specific examples of prospects who withheld information, introductions, or other signs of investment and commitment. List these examples below.

_____

_____

_____

_____

_____

_____

Did you win any of those deals? List wins below. Next to each win, explain how you changed the process.

_____

_____

_____

_____

_____

_____

_____

30

Action

Here is a checklist for harpooners to gauge the quality of their process on a whale deal. Apply it to your current whale deals and then work with your team to improve it.

☐ Do you know their buying process?

☐ Does it align with your sales process?

☐ Are you meeting the people who will be most affected by a change of providers?

☐ Are the right people committing to come to meetings?

☐ When you have a meeting scheduled, do people who committed to come actually show up?

☐ If they don't show up, have they notified you ahead of time in order to reschedule?

☐ Are they fully engaged with you?

☐ Do they challenge you with hard but relevant questions?

When your process is going well, you will have "yes" answers to these questions.

_____

_____

_____

_____

_____

info@thewhalehunters.com

www.thewhalehunters.com
© 2007-2016 The Whale Hunters, Inc.

"Perception is everything" and "Whales only believe what they see." Did you know that what the whale sees can be managed if you simply present your organization in the best possible light? We call this "Managing the Aperture of Perception."

32

Managing the Aperture of Perception

How can small companies position themselves to sell business to much larger companies? One key component of the sales process is what we call "the aperture of perception."

It's a photographic analogy. Simply stated, the person behind the camera deliberately selects the point of view, the scope of revelation, the interplay of background and foreground, the relative light and darkness. Just as there is artistry in setting up the photo shoot, there should
be artistry in your presentation to the prospect.

Your prospects will see you through the aperture – the opening – that you create. Your success differential is to create the aperture by deliberation, not by default. It's up to you to select all of the details that your prospect experiences.

We are not suggesting that you misrepresent your business. Rather, we suggest that you purposefully present in the best possible light the high points of your people, your promises, your processes, and your production. This presentation calls for systematic preparation and implementation.

Here's our list of the Top Ten Elements of your Aperture of Perception and our suggestions on how to manage them:

1. **Image:** Is your website pertinent and professional?

2. **Voice:** Have you prepared every receptionist to handle and route calls from your prospect?

3. **Knowledge:** Does every member of your team demonstrate deep knowledge of the prospect's business?

4. **Quality:** Is your proposal or statement of work correct, attentive to detail, attractive, and stylistically appropriate?

5. **Depth:** Are you engaging your subject matter experts in specific ways to support the sales process?

6. **Commitment:** Can your prospect observe a commitment to excellent delivery in all interactions with your company?

7. **Enthusiasm:** Does your entire village express a desire to serve this customer?

www.thewhalehunters.com
© 2007-2016 The Whale Hunters, Inc.   info@thewhalehunters.com

8. **Respect:** Can you ensure that all of your company's deliverables to the prospect are completed on time?

9. **Courtesy:** Will everyone on your team go the extra mile in arranging for site visits, conference calls, team meetings, and other events?

10. **Sincerity:** Will your prospect feel a sincere desire for their business from every encounter with your team members?

The measure of success for each of these criteria is not "good" or "bad," but "will it distinguish your firm from all other competitors"?

info@thewhalehunters.com
www.thewhalehunters.com
© 2007-2016 The Whale Hunters, Inc.

Reflection

Here is a checklist to assess your Aperture of Perception.

Perception	Control	Your Rating 1-5
Image	Website pertinent and professional	
Voice	Calls are answered and routed properly	
Knowledge	Every team member has deep knowledge of prospect	
Quality	Proposal is correct, attractive, appropriate	
Depth	Subject matter experts fully trained to support sales	
Commitment	Commitment to excel is evident in all interactions	
Enthusiasm	Entire village expresses a desire to serve this customer	
Respect	All deliverables are completed on time	
Courtesy	Calls, meetings, site visits handled properly	
Sincerity	Every encounter reinforces your team's desire to serve	

Action

Prioritize three top areas for improvement and assign responsibilities and due dates.

Area for improvement	Who is in charge of improvement	What are the signs of improvement	When is improvement to be visible
•	•	•	•
•	•	•	•
•	•	•	•
•	•	•	•
•	•	•	•
•	•	•	•
•	•	•	•
•	•	•	•

info@thewhalehunters.com

www.thewhalehunters.com

Placing second in poker is nothing more than being the first loser. The Whale Hunters abhor second place! Here we present the signs of "being played" by a whale and a few heavy-hitting tactics to stack the odds back in your favor.

www.thewhalehunters.com
© 2007-2016 The Whale Hunters, Inc.   info@thewhalehunters.com

Being Played by a Whale

Regular readers of *Whale Hunters Wisdom* are familiar with the idea of Texas Hold'em Poker and how to play that game with whales. Our point always is that Texas Hold'em players who win the most money play the fewest hands. They have learned how to fold early, often, and with confidence that if they had stayed in the game all the way to the end, they might have come in second. Second is the worst place to finish in poker because you've spent the most money to lose.

Great poker players entice their opponents to bet all of their chips and to finish second in one grand play. They accomplish this by giving the other player signs that he is winning when he is actually losing.

As whale hunters, we abhor coming in second. We don't want to launch that boat and expend all those resources only to come home without a whale. So we are big fans of folding, early, often, and with confidence. Yet whales are often very good at enticing you to play too long.

In the world of whale hunting, chips are resources, information, people, and time. The only way a whale can get you to put all of your best and brightest people, relationships, and efforts into a deal is to make you feel as if you are winning. However, if you knew you were losing, you would have folded a lot earlier instead of continuing to bet.

info@thewhalehunters.com

www.thewhalehunters.com
© 2007-2016 The Whale Hunters, Inc.

Why does a Buyers' Table keep you in the game when that whale is seriously interested in selecting a different company?

- Your ideas and concessions give it leverage with the finalist.

- The whale enjoys the free consulting.

- The company's process requires multiple bids.

- The whale is keeping its options open.

- Members of the table are reluctant to deliver bad news to you.

Well, then, how can you know when you are "being played?" Here are some signs:

1. **Delays and pings.** Early in a sales process, the key coin on the table is information. As the whale sends information to you, know that your firm is in a strong position. You can tell that deals are moving forward by the flow of information.

The danger sign to watch for is the promise delayed. If the whale commits to providing information but misses commitments, you do not occupy a winning position. The false positive is the "ping" you get from the whale: a hasty email or phone call with an apology for not getting information to you, or a promise for a best effort in the next week or so. Chances are the people who are winning are getting the necessary information well ahead of you.

40

2. **Push-offs.** In many complex deals, design meetings, process discussions, systems integration discussions, and other meetings are necessary before a final proposal can be made. The schedule for these meetings is often set early in the sales process, if only for the first of the meetings. If the meetings are scheduled and then pushed off, it is a good sign that other priorities, including your competitor, are interrupting the process.

3. **Collapse of the Buyers' Table.** Early in the buying process, access should be open between the subject matter experts in your boat and the members of the Buyer's Table. However, you can tell when a deal is going poorly when different members of your boat are reaching out to their Buyers' Table, but all of the answers come back through one person.

4. **Chasing the whale.** There is a difference between professional follow-up and desperate pursuit. When the frequency of response at all levels of the Buyers' Table and the boat begin to go on delay, then you know that you are losing. The whale is keeping you in the process, but has already begun the phase of developing final specifications with either the incumbent or the company that they will select that is not you.

5. **Quote the raven "nevermore."** When your raven goes cryptic, you are in trouble. Usually your harpooner will be keeping a regular dialog with the champion of your company inside the whale. The information will flow at a pretty predictable and favorable rate. When your raven begins to qualify her responses, not answer questions because of confidentiality, or limit your information, she is starting to pull back from you because she knows that you are losing the deal.

41

6. **Deadline delay.** When the company has selected its finalist but has not concluded the specifications and received final bidding from the preferred company, it may keep leverage on the preferred company by delaying the selection date. In this way, it creates doubt in the winner's mind and keeps its options open. If the deadline has been delayed, and you are not in negotiations with the buyer, you have probably lost. You are being told to be patient, but the fact is that your only chance is to be a "spoiler" and take a more radical approach to winning the deal, because at this point, you've lost.

So what to do?

Well, giving up is not necessarily the best step, even if it is the surest way to make certain not to spend any more resources. We recommend a few other options.

1. **Pull your boat together and consult with your shaman.** This is not the first time that he or she has been through this dance with a whale, and you can brainstorm some courses of action to get this hunt back on track. Allow the team, not the individual, to prevail.

2. **Change your key points of contact.** Do this, regardless of who, at the Buyers' Table or from your boat, is doing the majority of the communication at this step. It is not working. You may need to change up those relationships in order to change your progress. Face up to the possibility that someone on your boat is not the best fit with this whale.

42

3. **Use your Chief.** Sometimes the raven that helped to get you into a deal cannot help you close the deal. In this case, your most senior person needs to cultivate a direct and personal relationship with the highest person inside of the whale. These types of relationships, if managed correctly, can allow for a great deal of candor. On many occasions, we have advised our clients to make the high-risk call to the polar bear. Your Chief's question is simple: "Are we really in this deal, or are we just going through the motions?" Putting the polar bear on the spot will often yield more information than any other tactic can accomplish, but it can only be used once and only when the Chief has built a strong relationship with the polar bear.

Use these few tactics sparingly. If they don't produce the immediate results that you need, be prepared to walk away.

By definition, whales are much bigger than you. In the vernacular, you might say that they hold all the cards. But if you study the game, you'll know that it's not size that wins but an astute ability to fold, preserving your resources for the next deal.

Visit our website now to claim your free list of CEO membership organizations!
http://thewhalehunters.com/CEOlist

43

Reflection

With your team, brainstorm two or three prior lost deals with whale prospects. Complete this form for each example with "plays" that you recall on the whale's side.

Whale Prospect _____

"Play" Tactic	How We Knew
Delays	
Push-offs	
Collapse of Buyers' Table	
Frequency of Response	
Raven Disappears	
Deadline Delay	

44

Action

With your team, review a current deal in which you may have signs that the whale is playing. Complete this form any time a whale deal is stalling and you are not sure that they intend to move.

Whale Prospect _____

"Play" Tactic	What We Will Do
Delays	
Push-offs	
Collapse of Buyers' Table	
Frequency of Response	
Raven Disappears	
Deadline Delay	

info@thewhalehunters.com

www.thewhalehunters.com
© 2007-2016 The Whale Hunters, Inc.

In the Information Age, information abounds. Smart whales can easily learn about your company – and you about them. Read on to learn strategies for maintaining the balance and ensuring a level playing field throughout the sales process.

46

Whales are Smart

Marine scientists have learned recently that humpback whales have brain cells similar to those of human beings. That finding means either that they are as smart as we are, or that we are as smart as they! Regardless, for those of us who hunt whales, the idea of really smart whales is not new. Many of your prospective clients are going to be as smart about your company as you are about your prospects. Armed with Google tools, public records, and easy access to your company website, smart whales are looking as hard at you as you are at them.

In today's marketplace, whales are driven to know all about their supply chain. For that reason, internal buyers as well as procurement departments are becoming more sophisticated and demanding about the quality, timeliness, and depth of the information they request from potential vendors. Further, they can verify quickly the information that you provide in order to eliminate potential suppliers who are "puffing" their capabilities or testimonials. Just as it is in our best interest to get rid of whales that do not meet our criteria, the demands of the whale encourage buyers to limit their potential partner pool, quickly and often.

These new realities prompt me to ask a troubling question: What does a truly transparent sales process mean to a sales organization? If our prospects can learn as much about us as they want, how do we control the ways in which we differentiate ourselves? How do we properly pace the mutual discovery process if the initial meeting becomes a simple verification of what the whale has already learned about us?

www.thewhalehunters.com
© 2007-2016 The Whale Hunters, Inc.

info@thewhalehunters.com

As whale hunters, we have learned with our clients over time that *information* is neither good nor bad – it just is. How cleverly your company gathers information, how fearlessly you confront it, and how rigorously you demand it are the methods by which excellent whale hunters and excellent whale prospects cull their ideal partners from the rest. For this reason, don't assume that a prospect that seeks to know a lot about your company will gain an upper hand on you. However, there are some important rules for companies wanting to leverage an open market:

- **Know as much about you as your whales do.** It may seem simple, but it is worth spending energy on the following items:

  - Run a Dun & Bradstreet report on yourself. If your prospect can look at the public information on your financial history, you should know what it is. Take the necessary steps to correct inaccuracies or to improve your financial rating.

  - Check your own website for accuracy and timely information. We recently worked with a client that had discontinued updating the press room on its website. In a prospect meeting concerning the firm's ability to address e-commerce needs, the more-than-one-year information gap on the website became a hotly contested objection which our client could not overcome.

  - Know what is written about you and who is writing it. These days, it is as easy as setting a Google alert to have all articles containing your company name be sent to you. No complicated clipping services are needed, and you will know what is being written within a very short time of its publication.

- Know what your clients are saying about you. Many companies conduct surface-level customer satisfaction surveys. But more meaningful customer loyalty and satisfaction are best measured by answers to questions about a company's willingness to recommend you to others. You must know what your customers think and what they will say.

- **Provide information to your prospects that is not easily available to them.** Whatever they can find on the Internet is by definition "public" knowledge. Give your prospective customers something different to educate them about your credibility. Here are some ideas:

  - Offer an overwhelming number of testimonials. Although these are great on the website, an in-person stack of testimonials on original letterhead with titles and contact information will provide a sense of assurance unavailable through public material.

  - Provide your company's performance trend lines to whales. Most press releases and other articles refer to events in your company's history. If you offer more in the form of context over time, you will increase the respect that whales will have for your lineage and growth. Remember, you need to alleviate the whale's fear before you can explain your advantages.

info@thewhalehunters.com

www.thewhalehunters.com
© 2007-2016 The Whale Hunters, Inc.

- **Do not waste the whale's time.** If it becomes apparent your whale is very knowledgeable about your firm, acknowledge their effort and focus your valuable time with them.

  - Thank the buyers for doing their homework and compliment them on their willingness to examine their partners carefully.

  - Explain that you also have investigated them and have decided that a potential partnership is a good idea.

  - Ask them to explain what they have learned about you so that you will not be redundant in your discussions but will have the opportunity to answer questions, explain confusing information, or correct misperceptions.

  - Answer all of their questions honestly and clearly. This is your one chance to demonstrate the integrity of your firm, and candor will make a difference. The whale may know all that you know and want to test your willingness to engage them in an honest fashion.

  - Move the discussion to the needs of the target firm and reference your capabilities only in the context of solving specific problems or helping them to capitalize on specific opportunities.

Today's open marketplace creates a level playing field. However, many companies are accustomed to masking their mistakes or using only canned presentations in their first conversations with a whale. Those practices put off the whale and, worse, suggest that they have things to hide.

Understanding that knowledge gathering goes both ways allows a whale hunter to prepare for the intelligent whale and meet it, brain to brain and mind to mind.

info@thewhalehunters.com

www.thewhalehunters.com
© 2007-2016 The Whale Hunters, Inc.

Reflection

Do you know what whales can discover about you? Do a search and write key points here:

_____

_____

_____

What pages or sections of your website are outmoded? List them here and set a review and revision date.

Website Problem	Revision Target Date

What do your customers say about you? Ask them, and write down three key responses.

_____

_____

_____

52

Action

Create a rich library of testimonials and case studies. List your first five targets here:

_____

_____

_____

_____

_____

Create performance trend charts to use in your collateral materials to put events in context. These might feature annual revenue, number of new customers per years, average size of sale, or number of industry awards and recognition. For example, here is a simple revenue chart [if you don't want to share actual numbers, show percentage of growth year over year]:

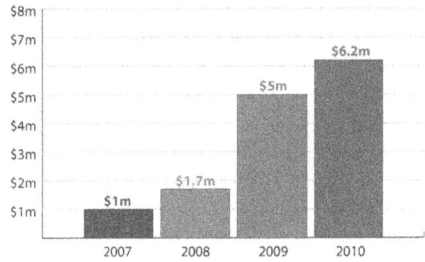

2007	$1m
2008	$1.7m
2009	$5m
2010	$6.2m

53

www.thewhalehunters.com
© 2007-2016 The Whale Hunters, Inc.

Of course the occasional whale hunting failure occurs. But why? Several factors, alone or in combination, contribute to such negative results. Understanding and proactively avoiding these factors translates into an almost assured success. Find out how.

Whale Hunting Failures

Recently we were meeting with a prospect who asked us, "Have you ever had an occasion when whale hunting was not successful?"

The answer, of course, is yes.

Just as the Inuit did not land a whale on every hunt, so modern businesses will experience at least an occasional failure. Whale hunting is a growth strategy that requires the coordination of many interdependent elements. If any one element is missing or not working well, the probability of failure increases.

These examples illustrate reasons for a failed hunt or a failed hunting process:

1. **The wrong whale.** The first phase in the whale hunting model is "know the whale" – define the odds-in-your-favor whale to hunt and harvest. One of our clients identified that their best whales would be of a size between $500,000 and $1.5 million in first year annual revenue. They spotted a whale prospect, launched a boat, and discovered that the opportunity was actually $5 million. They were ecstatic – what a great whale opportunity for growth for the company! However, the process for identifying their perfect whale had been rigorous and accurate: they were really best able to serve a whale no larger than $1.5 million. Entrepreneurial enthusiasm caused them to violate their own target filter parameters. This whale almost killed them, taking almost 15 months before they could digest it and start making money.

   Whale hunting works. Apply the system and you will land whales. Just remember to get only the whales you want.

www.thewhalehunters.com
© 2007-2016 The Whale Hunters, Inc.

2. **No Chief on the boat.** We hear many CEOs complain, "Look at our client list. It seems that I have to bring in all the big accounts. Why can't my salespeople bring in big accounts?"

The fact is that whales demand that the CEO be involved in the relationship for a whale-sized opportunity. The whale knows that it represents a big opportunity and that the work will demand a high level of resources and attention from your company. It wants to look the CEO in the eye during the sales process in order to feel comfortable.

Furthermore, almost every new whale that you land will significantly change your company. You will add new processes, equipment, personnel, technology, or some other enterprise-changing element to support the whale. The CEO has to be a part of the whale hunt in order to envision and implement these changes.

In our experience, when the CEO of a small to mid-size business that is whale hunting does not participate actively and in the appropriate role during the hunt, that company's whale hunting activity does not produce the outcomes that the CEO was hoping for.

3. **No scout.** When companies are small, salespeople are expected to perform all nine phases of the sales process themselves – what we call scouting, hunting, and harvesting functions. As a company grows, it often segments sales activities into "hunters" and "farmers," which means that hunters both scout and hunt and farmers both hunt and harvest. But when a company chooses

to whale hunt, we believe that the three core areas of scouting, hunting, and harvesting are unique, each requiring dedicated personnel, tools, and processes to be effective.

One company with which we worked stuck to the hunter/farmer model, preferring not to invest in scouting resources. As a result, the hunters quickly reached their capacity for whale hunting, and there was little capacity to grow without hiring additional hunters. The capacity threshold is expensive. This company hunts whales; however, its growth is slower than it could be if they allocated the resources to the process. In the end, this strategy is penny-wise and pound-foolish.

4. **No boat.** "Seven people on one side of the table and me on the other; it felt less like a sales call and more like a firing squad." This we heard from a harpooner at a client company. We are helping that company implement the whale hunting process. They have recognized that by sending one salesperson out to whale-sized opportunities, they were scaring their whales.

Whales learn from harpooners (your sales staff) why they should work with your firm. However, to make them feel safe and willing to work with you, they need to understand what and how. Your boat – the subject matter experts in your company who speak at a peer-to-peer level with their counterparts in the whale – best provides this information.

Your investment in training and using the right number of operationally knowledgeable people will help you land whales and will give you a competitive edge over competitors that are comparable in size to you.

5. **No village.** "Our village pushes whales away from the shore when they happen to beach themselves." You may think we're exaggerating, but we have heard this lament from harpooners countless times. Companies that try to adopt whale hunting only as a sales strategy, rather than a culture change, find themselves with whales lining up in the bay and rotting on the shore.

In the world of whale hunting, a big new contract often includes ramp-up provisions that allow the whale to evaluate your key performance indicators in the early stages of the agreement, after which they will determine how quickly to implement the full contract. If your village is not completely engaged and committed, their performance will keep the whale on the shore, no matter how effective your sales process has been. Whale hunting is a way of life that allows everyone in the organization to win. It is a cultural change implemented in a process-based way.

So, can whale hunting fail? You bet. It can fail by being successful in landing the wrong whales, it can fail by partial implementation, and it can fail from a lack of organizational commitment in a variety of ways.

But as your company learns to avoid these pitfalls, your success is almost assured. To minimize failure, give rigorous attention to your preparation before the hunt and your analysis after the hunt.

www.thewhalehunters.com
© 2007-2016 The Whale Hunters, Inc.

info@thewhalehunters.com

Reflection

With your team, identify key opportunities that failed. Did any of the reasons in this article apply to any of your failed deals?

Deal That Failed	Reasons the Deal Failed

info@thewhalehunters.com

www.thewhalehunters.com

Action

Identify three specific areas of improvement that would reduce your number of failed deals. With your team, determine what needs to be improved, who is responsible for leading the initiative, and when the change should be implemented.

Need for Change	Who is Responsible for Leading Change Initiative	When Should This Change be Implemented

info@thewhalehunters.com

Killer whales should not swim through your target filter criteria; they declare in advance how dangerous they are, and they move through the sales process at an unacceptable pace. Steer clear of them at all cost!

info@thewhalehunters.com   www.thewhalehunters.com
© 2007-2016 The Whale Hunters, Inc.

Avoid Killer Whales

Not every whale is a good whale. We know that the killer whale is the most dangerous of all whales. Why? After all, it's smaller than many of its brethren, it is not easily disguised because of its distinctive markings, and the number of its kind is relatively small. But it is feared because it does something no other whale does: it kills other whales!

A killer whale kills other whales by exhausting them and then holding them underwater until they drown. It does not take a bite out of its victim, but rather slowly and methodically wears it down until its prey sees death as a relief. You can probably look back on your history with large prospects and spot the killer whales among the group.

Killer whales pose a tremendous risk to your firm. If your team engages with the wrong whale, it will wear you out, drown you in your own wasted effort, and yield no prize for the village. But how do you know whether a whale is a killer whale?

1. First, if a whale does not meet your criteria for an ideal piece of business, it may be a killer whale. Maybe you are tempted to consider business which is too big to handle, or will take you in a direction that you have not decided to go, or fails to meet other requirements that you've established for considering a new opportunity. Greed gets in the way of common sense, or you fear that this whale is the only whale in the ocean, and you stop being diligent in your assessment. If you want to gain the benefits of whale hunting, your firm must stick to its target filter.

2. Second, in early meetings a killer whale will often broadcast its intentions. Companies like WalMart have developed a reputation for being aggressive negotiators and difficult clients. Executives from this firm begin their meetings with prospective partners by laying out their process for working with new companies. Whales will often tell you in advance that they are difficult to work with, or that they use only procurement for final negotiations, or that they do not sign mutually protective contracts and will not consider a long term relationship. If these issues are clear flags in your target filter, eliminate that whale from your list and move on.

3. Third, if your pursuit of a whale is progressing too quickly or too slowly, you may be pursuing a killer. If the whale is dragging you through the process at a breakneck pace, you need to determine why that is. Prospective clients do not always publish their agendas or internal issues. Stick to your whale hunting process and take the time necessary to decide whether or not you want to work with the firm. If they insist on moving more quickly than you believe is prudent, it is time to leave.

However, moving too slowly is equally bad. If you have carefully designed and tested your sales process, you know that it works for you. You are more likely to make bad decisions when you are under pressure or feel the need to move things along more quickly. That's why killer whales may stall the process to see if you will offer a better deal in the fear of losing this one. Or they will use your precious intellectual capital to develop their own solution or to educate your competitor. Have a frank and candid conversation with your prospects to set clear expectations about the process and milestones. If the whale rejects your process, have the courage to hunt a different whale.

Whale hunting always requires courage, not only the courage to hunt, but often the courage to forego a hunt. In many ways, the whales you let go are more valuable to you than the ones you bring in. Wasted efforts are expensive and discouraging to the village. The village will lose faith in the process if it is unable to trust that the whales being targeted will be good for the firm.

Be careful, be courageous, and stay away from killer whales!

www.thewhalehunters.com
© 2007-2016 The Whale Hunters, Inc.

info@thewhalehunters.com

Reflection

Have you ever landed a killer whale? With your team, brainstorm the list of qualities that made it a killer [for example, mismatch with the Target Filter, warning signs ignored, process problems]:

-

-

-

-

-

-

-

-

-

-

Action

Based on the "killer qualities" that you identified on the previous page, make a list of steps you could take to avoid killer whales in the future.

1.

2.

3.

4.

5.

www.thewhalehunters.com
© 2007-2016 The Whale Hunters, Inc.

info@thewhalehunters.com

"Ship-shape, everyone, and all hands on deck!" Once you've convinced a whale to visit your facility, you stand a better-than-awesome chance to close that whale-sized deal. Here are tips for ensuring a standing ovation at your Big Show... every time.

www.thewhalehunters.com
© 2007-2016 The Whale Hunters, Inc.

Company's Coming!

Remember the first time you asked your sweetheart to dinner – which you'd cook, at your house? And you got "Yes!" for an answer? After the shock wore off, you probably swung into full preparation mode, but not before getting some advice from your favorite Aunt Ruth, who said wisely, "Now remember, dear: Don't just set the table. Set the mood!"

Heeding that advice has yielded big dividends for millions of lovebirds through the ages. And it does in whale hunting, too. When you invite your whale to visit, you want to set a mood for romance and leave the whale feeling unafraid of continuing the courtship.

A critical step in the whale hunt is the day when the whale pays you a visit. By this time, you have carefully navigated the stages of qualifying, first meeting, and proof of concept sharing – progressively discovering key information about the whale and revealing pertinent details about yourselves. You know who is at the Buyers' Table and you've populated your boat with appropriate subject matter experts. Through the process, you have gained a clearer understanding of the whale's needs and generated specific ideas for how your company will meet those needs.

Yet the whale still feels that nagging fear – fear of change, conflict, mistakes, or work – all of the above. Working with your company or implementing your solution just looks scary – too risky, too untested – from the whale's perspective.

So when company's coming to your facility, do everything you can to mitigate the whale's fear. Prepare with precision, implement flawlessly, and follow-up with speed and care. During and after the visit, take every opportunity to press into service the four fear busters – people, process, technology, and experience. Anything less could worsen the whale's fear and send it comfortably back to that same old way of doing business that you are trying to crack.

We call this visit the "Big Show." Implementing your version of the Big Show can have powerful outcomes in closing your whale hunting deals.

Prepare with precision

When a whale visits your company headquarters, all of your employees should be prepared to orchestrate the Big Show. Face-to-face conversations should be relevant and knowledgeable. You will want your employees to be able to demonstrate the parallels between the current and proposed conditions in the whale. That understanding will help the whale buyers to feel comfort and safety.

But don't stop there. Consider the power of the visit when everyone at your location knows the whale, knows the date and time of the visit, and understands the importance of the Big Show to the company's success and therefore to their personal success.

info@thewhalehunters.com

www.thewhalehunters.com
© 2007-2016 The Whale Hunters, Inc.

- Announce the whale's visit to all employees well ahead of the visit.

- Send a dossier to everyone who will touch the whale.

- Prepare and distribute two versions of the agenda – planned to the 15 minute increment.

  - A detailed backstage agenda for participants from your organization

  - A front-stage agenda for all whale invitees

- Pair your subject matter experts with whale counterparts so the pairs may deal with specific issues and agenda items.

- Assign and communicate clear roles and responsibilities to all participants.

- Remind all employees the day before to dress appropriately and clean their areas.

- Check and double-check infrastructure – lighting, technology, parking, internal operations, seating arrangements, name badges – to ensure working order on the day.

- Demonstrate visual indicators of control and performance: display customer testimonials on mobile whiteboards, illustrate department performance with strategically placed charts and graphs, position computer screens and dashboards so that the visitors can see them.

- Rehearse, rehearse, rehearse.

Implement flawlessly

From the receptionist's smile to the Q&A session, from the software demonstration to the very last handshake, let every message say to the whale, "We are capable."

- Greet the invitees by name; welcome the whale with a big sign in the reception area.

- Follow the agenda and seating chart.

- Provide appropriate refreshments throughout the day, ensuring that the workspace is set and re-set to be continually fresh and welcoming.

- Ensure that your presenters are prepared for two important functions: to gather information and to demonstrate knowledge and capability.

- If you are presenting, make clear your understanding of the whale's needs .

- Highlight your tools, processes, systems, and other methods that mitigate fears.

- Involve other subject matter experts at appropriate moments to discuss their expertise.

- Answer the whale's questions; acknowledge those you can't answer and commit to answering them promptly.

- Thank the whale for visiting and agree upon next steps together.

info@thewhalehunters.com   www.thewhalehunters.com
© 2007-2016 The Whale Hunters, Inc.

Follow-up with speed and care

- Answer all pending questions.

- Follow-through on all commitments.

- Thank and provide feedback to all internal participants.

- Discuss and document lessons learned for continuous improvement .

- Tell everyone the outcomes as soon as you know.

We've been privileged to work for a number of clients who have honed their Big Show for prospects. These companies have a near 100% close rate on whale-sized deals when they are able to host the prospect's buying team at their facility.

Aunt Ruth would probably say, "An ounce of prevention is worth a pound of cure," wouldn't she? When it comes to the Big Show, she'd be right, of course. Careful preparation on your part delivers a "fear-free" mood on the whale's part – every time.

Reflection

Do you invite prospects to visit your facility or a "showplace" installation?

_____

_____

_____

If you don't, should you?

_____

_____

_____

If you do, do you have a fail safe process?

• Script

_____

_____

• Training

_____

_____

• Imagination

_____

_____

73

Action

Create your detailed script for a whale to visit you. Assign responsibilities. [If visiting you is not appropriate or relevant, plan the "Road Show" in which your team visits them.

Stop on Tour	Who is Presenting	Key Points	Props, Examples

The Whale Hunters Glossary

The Whale Hunters draw upon the rich legend and lore of the Inuit whale hunters of the far northwest to engage executives in a new way of thinking: for explosive growth, hunt whales.

Ambergris - Rare and priceless substance produced deep within the gut of a sperm whale. The Whale Hunters use this term to represent additional value to be located within existing key accounts.

Beach - During the Beach phase (one of nine in The Whale Hunters Process™), you prepare and present the intake document, develop a harvest map, and commit to performance metrics.

Boat - The team of villagers who hunt and capture a specific whale. The team includes a harpooner, shaman, and several oarsmen, subject matter experts (SMEs) who are needed to close a complex sale. SMEs on each boat represent all areas of the company. The village Chief may also be involved.

Buyers' Table - Those at the whale company who will be affected by your company's solution and participate in the buying decision. Key positions at this table (among others) are the polar bear (economic buyer) and caribou (technical buyers).

Capture - The Capture phase, one of nine in The Whale Hunters Process™, involves those activities traditionally associated with "closing": finalizing the proposal, closing the deal, negotiating terms, and completing the contract.

info@thewhalehunters.com

www.thewhalehunters.com

Caribou - Individuals at the whale company - often technical buyers - who participate at the Buyers' Table and influence the buying decision; however, their position only allows them to say "no."

Chief - President, CEO, Founder or other person identified as responsible for the company's growth and delivery of profits. This person is responsible for ensuring that the village is ready to harvest whales, re-calibrates the Target Filter, and has final say as to whether a boat hunts or not.

Celebrate - During Celebrate (one of nine phases in The Whale Hunters Process™), your company conducts an internal post-harvest review, documents and integrates lessons learned, and determines ways to celebrate the whale (i.e. make the whale aware of both your company's appreciation for it and your company's commitment to your ongoing relationship).

Culture - The shared history of what has made your company successful. As the village transforms into a whale-hunting village, certain cultural beliefs change but core values can be maintained and reinforced.

Dossier (Scouting and Hunting) - Document used to communicate research information about a whale from the scout to the harpooner and shaman.

Eel - Gatekeepers, deal spoilers, and nay-sayers at the whale company who work to prevent any sort of change.

76

Gap Analysis - The results of an analysis the village performs comparing the needs of a particular whale against the village's current ability to meet those needs. Areas such as legal, finance, technology, operations, and logistics are typically included in such analyses.

Harpoon - Harpoon is one of the nine phases in The Whale Hunters Process™. During this phase, the whale hunter gets the whale's attention using a combination of an effective contact approach and a well-crafted message. Your company completes a needs assessment of the whale and designs and delivers a presentation to put forward your credentials and convey your understanding of the whale's needs.

Harpooner - Salesperson who hunts whales. The harpooner is responsible for identifying the key decision-makers inside of a whale, qualifying the whale, generating interest in the whale, and bringing the whale through the sales process.

Harvesting - This term refers to all activities that the boat and the village perform from the point of agreement with a client through a defined period of time (usually the first 90 days of the contract).

Honor - One of nine phases of The Whale Hunters Process™, Honor is the period of time surrounding that point when actual production or service delivery begins.

Intake and Setup - This term refers to specific activities the village and boat perform during the whale harvesting process. These activities are usually focused on an intense period of interaction just prior to the harvest through the first 30 days of contract performance.

Know - One of the nine phases of The Whale Hunters Process™, Know focuses on knowing your market, your strengths, your competition, and the ideal whales that you want to hunt.

Oarsmen - Key subject matter experts (SMEs) who are identified by the shamans and the village Chief to participate in the sales process on the boat. These individuals have specific knowledge of elements of the products/services that the company is selling and contribute to bringing the whale into the boat during The Whale Hunters Process™.

Polar Bear - Target decision-maker (also referred to as the economic buyer) at the whale company who can say "yes" or "no."

Process Map - Visual and narrative representation of the series of choreographed activities in the village's whale hunting process. It includes every element of the nine-phase process - from Knowing the Whale to Celebrating the Whale - in the detailed series of steps that are defined for a particular village.

Raven - Advocates of your company whose wisdom is sought after (and appreciated) by the shaman. Ravens take many shapes and forms. Some ravens are key insiders and associates of your company. Others are your guides on the customer side. Still another type of raven is a compensated intermediary.

Ride - During the Ride phase, you recruit and train subject matter experts to join your hunt, you analyze the whale's buying group, and you stage the whale's visit to your facility. Ride is one of nine phases in The Whale Hunters Process™.

Scout - Marketing person who performs research on whales, generates dossiers on whales, monitors the market for "whale sign," and supports the harpooners as per the shaman's direction.

Searching for Ambergris (SFA) - A specific process and set of tools for capturing more business with the village's existing whale accounts.

Seek - One of nine phases in The Whale Hunters Process™, Seek refers to the process by which your company collects, collates, and tracks account-specific information, including a prospect's readiness to buy. The shaman and harpooners use this information to decide which whales to hunt and how and when to hunt them.

Sew - This phase represents that time between a verbal or even contractual agreement to buy and the actual delivery of services. It is one of nine phases in The Whale Hunters Process™.

Shaman - The direct supervisor of a group of harpooners. The shaman is responsible for training the members of the boat, facilitating the whale hunting process, communicating with the tribe, and managing the tracking process.

Subject Matter Expert (SME) - Villager with responsibilities in hunting and harvesting a specific whale. SMEs represent such areas as research and development, legal, human resources, information technology, operations, manufacturing,shipping, and others. They are selected as oarsmen when a particular boat is launched.

Target Filter - The target filter is used as the evaluation chart for all prospective whales in the marketplace. Using the elements provided in the target filter, a score is given to each prospect whale and that score determines whether and when the village hunts.

The Whale Hunters Process™ - an integrated sales process by which a company is able to sell and service massive accounts.

Village - All members of the company in all departments.

Whale - A sales prospect for a company that is whale hunting. The prospect is distinct from other sales prospects because its meets pre-defined criteria of size and desirability as a client.

Whale Chart - Environmental scan of the marketplace and its inhabitants. This document identifies and qualifies the various opportunities in the marketplace by their desirable characteristics as a client.

Visit our website now to claim your free list of CEO membership organizations!
http://thewhalehunters.com/CEOlist

80

Also Available from The Whale Hunters

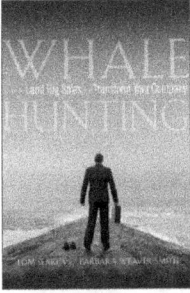

Whale Hunting is required reading for anyone who is going after the big fish in a market. Engaging, practical, and well organized, it is simply the best book on major account selling out there. Someone once said that confidence is going after Moby Dick in a rowboat and bringing the mayonnaise. *Whale Hunting* gives you the tools to pursue big deals with that kind of confidence.

~ Keith R. McFarland, author of *The Breakthrough Company: How Everyday Companies Become Extraordinary Performers*

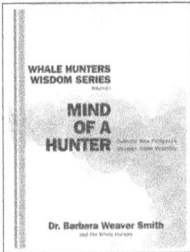

Mind of a Hunter reinforces the need for focus during a whale hunt. Each villager must know what each Inuit whale hunter knew: the whale is worth the trouble. No amount of distraction, fear, boredom, or nostalgia can be allowed to clutter the minds of the whale hunters eager to capture an account that will move your company to the next level.

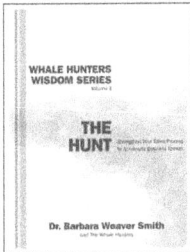

The Hunt introduces you to some of the unexpected ways a whale company can slip from the grasp of those small companies that are not able to hold the right tension on the harpoon line. Don't let the whale slip away from you. Learn the ways of the whale, the wind, and the water.

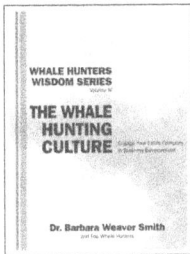

Whale Hunting Culture demonstrates that the entire village must be ready to harvest the whale as soon as you beach it—meaning the contract is signed. This volume offers methods to ensure that you can encourage a fast-growth culture that can properly deliver your services to a whale account.

81

WHALE HUNTERS WISDOM SERIES: RIDING THE WHALE   Also Available from The Whale Hunters

. . . .

Whale Hunting with Global Accounts: Four Critical Business Sales Strategies to Win Global Customers

By Dr. Barbara Weaver Smith

Discover the four critical sales strategies to win global customers, whether you're a seasoned global seller or just putting your toes into the ocean, a CEO or a sales manager. Featuring insights from interviews with fourteen global sales practitioners.

"Barbara Weaver Smith does it again! In her new book, **Whale Hunting with Global Accounts: Four Critical Strategies**, *she weaves in foundational concepts from her timeless book,* **Whale Hunting: How to Land Big Sales and Transform Your Company** *but adds a global bent. By capitalizing on the experience of fourteen experts (I was especially honored to be part of this elite group) she is able to analyze and address the many issues associated with landing and supporting global customers. If your company plans to expand your sales reach into global markets, I would suggest digesting every word of this book – it will save you countless hours and springboard your efforts to building a successful and sustainable global sales program."*

Lisa D. Magnuson
TOP Line Account™ Deal Coach
Top Line Sales

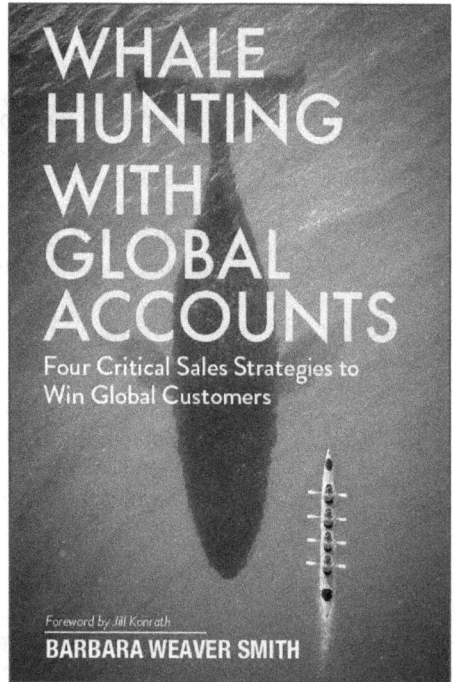

WHALE
HUNTING
WITH
GLOBAL
ACCOUNTS
Four Critical Sales Strategies to
Win Global Customers

Foreword by Jill Konrath
BARBARA WEAVER SMITH

82

Notes

www.thewhalehunters.com
© 2007-2016 The Whale Hunters, Inc.

Notes

Visit our website now to claim your free list of CEO membership organizations!
http://thewhalehunters.com/CEOlist

Whale Hunters Wisdom, Volume III: Riding the Whale

The Whale Hunters
3054 East Bartlett Place
Chandler, AZ 85249
www.thewhalehunters.com
info@thewhalehunters.com

Dr. Barbara Weaver Smith is available to speak to your organization about whale hunting, sales process development and integration, and accelerated cultural transformation. Contact The Whale Hunters at 480.584.4012 for more information.

www.ingramcontent.com/pod-product-compliance
Lightning Source LLC
Chambersburg PA
CBHW060638210326
41520CB00010B/1650